MY FIRST LOOK AT WEATHER

Wind blows hot-air balloons around

Wind

NATE LEBOUTILLIER

CREATIVE EDUCATION

Published by Creative Education

123 South Broad Street, Mankato, Minnesota 56001

Creative Education is an imprint of The Creative Company

Designed by Rita Marshall

Photographs by Alamy (PHOTOTAKE Inc., Peter Stroumtsos), Bonnie Sue Photography,

CLEO Photography, Getty Images (Adam Jones), JLM Visuals (Richard P. Jacobs), KAC

Productions (Larry Ditto), Sally McCrae Kuyper, Tom Myers, Tom Stack & Associates

(Dr. Scott Norquay, Brian Parker, Inga Spence)

Copyright © 2007 Creative Education

Printed in the United States of America

Library of Congress Cataloging-in-Publication Data

LeBoutillier, Nate. Wind / by Nate LeBoutillier.

p. cm. — (My first look at weather)

Includes index.

ISBN-13 : 978-1-58341-452-1

I. Wind—Juvenile literature. I. Title. II. Series.

QC931.4.L43 2006   551.51'8—dc22   2005037235

First edition 9 8 7 6 5 4 3 2 1

WIND

WIND EVERYWHERE

Wind blows and swirls. It whistles and moans. Wind pushes sailboats and turns windmills. Wind lifts up kites. When it is hot outside, wind can cool people down. Strong wind can also damage things on Earth and even harm people.

People usually cannot see wind, because it is **invisible**. Wind is air that is moving. Sometimes wind helps make the sky beautiful.

Wind can push sailboats very fast

Wind pushes clouds around. When the sun comes up or goes down, the clouds can block sunlight. The sky turns red, purple, orange, or other colors. It looks like a big, colorful painting.

What Is Wind?

The sun causes wind. The middle part of Earth is called the equator (*ee-KWAY-ter*). The sun heats the equator and makes it hot. The North Pole and South Pole are farther away from the sun. They are very cold.

Wind blowing 55 miles (90 km)
per hour (as fast as a car on
the highway) can knock down trees.

TREE LEAVES BLOW AROUND ON WINDY DAYS

Hot air is light. It **expands** and rises. Cold air is heavy. It **contracts** and falls. When hot air mixes with cold air, the cooler air scoots under the warmer air. This makes wind.

Wind carries different types of air. Wind carries hot and cold air. But it also carries wet air, dry air, fast-moving air, and slow-moving air. This makes different kinds of weather.

Long ago, some people thought that
Earth and the sky were gods. They
thought winds were the gods' children!

Harmful Wind

Sometimes wind can be very strong. When wind gets wild, storms happen. Hurricanes or cyclones are windstorms that start out in the ocean. They spin water and waves onto land.

Tornadoes are windstorms that come down from clouds to pick up dirt and dust. They can be very scary and powerful. Some tornadoes pick up trees and houses or even animals and people!

Tornadoes usually happen in
the spring or summer. Most appear
in the middle of the United States.

Blizzards are windstorms that blow snow and cold air so hard that it can be hard to see! Every year, some people around the world get hurt or even killed by windstorms.

HELPFUL WIND

Wind can help people in many ways, too. Wind that blows through windmills creates **electricity**. Electricity gives people energy. Many things in houses use energy, such as TVs, washing machines, and hair dryers.

Sometimes winds act like

mini-tornadoes in dry places.

They are called dust devils.

Wind can be used to help people travel, too. Wind can push sailboats, ships, and airplanes. Some cars even use wind to make themselves go! Wind that makes a bad storm can also push the storm away.

Airplanes use the wind so
they can fly faster from
one place to another.

WIND CAN HELP AIRPLANES FLY FAST

THESE WINDMILLS MAKE LOTS OF ELECTRICITY

Whether wind is helping people or causing problems, one thing is for sure. All around the world, the wind is always blowing!

THERE IS WIND ALL AROUND THE WORLD

Hands-on: Wind Spinner

Make a spinner to watch the power of the wind!

What You Need

A pin

Scissors

A sharpened pencil with eraser

A square piece of construction paper

What You Do

1. Draw lines from corner to corner on your paper. Punch a small hole with the pencil tip at the point where the lines cross.
2. Cut along each line, stopping about an inch (2.5 cm) from the hole.
3. Make a pin hole in the top left corner of each flap. Fold each punched corner toward the center hole.
4. Line up the holes. Push the pin through them and into the side of the eraser.

Hold your spinner facing the wind and watch it go!

A SPINNER SPINS FASTEST IN A STRONG WIND

Index

Words to Know

contracts—gets smaller or tighter

electricity—a kind of energy that turns on lights and makes machines run

expands—gets bigger or spreads out

invisible—something that cannot be seen

Read More

Cobb, Vicki. *I Face the Wind*. New York: Harper Collins Publishers, 2003.

Jennings, Terry. *Wind*. North Mankato, Minn.: Chrysalis Education, 2004.

Schaefer, Lola M. *A Windy Day*. Mankato, Minn.: Capstone Press, 2000.

Explore the Web

Energy Kids' Page—Wind Energy http://www.eia.doe.gov/kids/energyfacts/sources/renewable/wind.html

Weather Dude http://www.wxdude.com/

Weather Wiz Kids http://www.weatherwizkids.com